Skills for
SOCIAL SUCCESS

Written by Meg Greve

Content Consultant
Taylor K. Barton, LPC
School Counselor

Rourke
Educational Media

rourkeeducationalmedia.com

*Scan for Related Titles
and Teacher Resources*

www.rourkeeducationalmedia.com

PHOTO CREDITS: Cover: © Christopher Futcher; page 4: © GlobalStock; page 5, 7, 8, 13: © kali9; page 9: © Paz Ruiz Luque; page 11: © Juanmonino; page 12, 15, 17: © fstop123; page 14: © 1MoreCreative; page 16: © William Perugini; page 19: © Elena Elisseeva; page 21: © sturti; page 22: © Jane norton

Edited by Precious McKenzie

Cover and Interior Design by Tara Raymo

Library of Congress PCN Data

Skills for Social Success / Meg Greve
(Social Skills)
ISBN 978-1-62169-905-7 (hard cover) (alk. paper)
ISBN 978-1-62169-800-5 (soft cover)
ISBN 978-1-62717-011-6 (e-Book)
Library of Congress Control Number: 2013937300

Rourke Educational Media
Printed in the United States of America,
North Mankato, Minnesota

Also Available as:

rourkeeducationalmedia.com

customersevice@rourkeeducationalmedia.com • PO Box 643328 Vero Beach, Florida 32964

TABLE OF CONTENTS

Trying to figure out a long division problem is hard, but sometimes dealing with your social life at school can be even harder. Figuring out friendships, managing time, and learning about yourself are all important parts of growing up. Believe it or not, everyone feels just like you do. The trick is figuring out how to deal with it all and feel good while doing it.

Super Social Tip

Keep a positive attitude about yourself and things that interest you. There are many people with similar interests who would be happy to get to know you!

The most important person in your social circle is you. This does not mean that you should always get your way when you are with your friends, or that you get to be the one who makes every social decision. What this means is that if you take care of yourself, believe in who you are, and be yourself at all times, you will find people who want to be your friend.

Do you have special interests or **hobbies**? Now is the time to pursue those activities. It is easy to be friends with someone who has the same interests. Share your hobbies with others who show an interest in what you are doing.

Super Social Tip

Take a risk and join a club or team that you may not know a lot about. This is a great opportunity to learn a new skill or meet some new people.

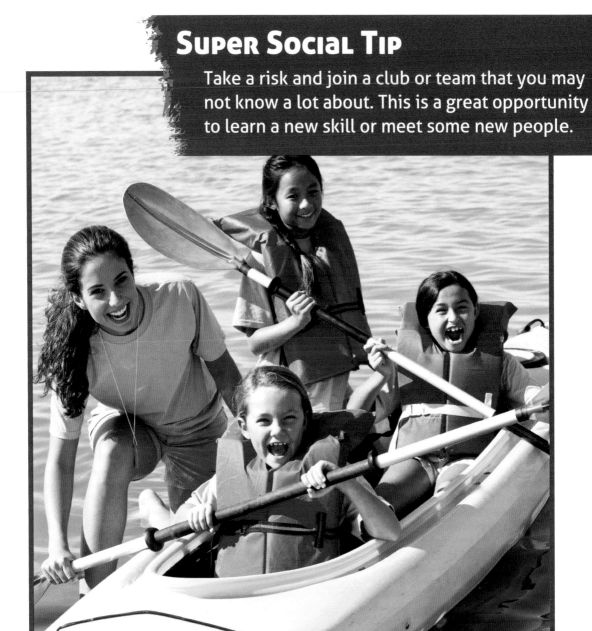

Do not worry if all of your friends do not share similar interests. It is also a good idea to form relationships with people who are different from you. Be sure to stick with what you like, and do not let others pressure you to be different than who you are. Focus on doing things that you enjoy.

MAKING FRIENDS

Promise yourself to remain true to who you are and you will be ready to make some friends. Don't change your beliefs or your interests to fit in with others. The easiest way to make friends is to join clubs or teams. You are sure to meet with these people at least once a week at meetings or practice. You will have the chance to talk and get to know one another in a relaxed way.

Super Social Tip

Stop gossip in its tracks. Think before you talk. Do not say something about someone else that you wouldn't say right to them. People will like and trust you if they know you are not a gossip.

Making friends can feel scary. You may have to take a chance and be the first one to start a **conversation**. Most people probably feel a little **nervous**. They will be relieved that you are the one who took that chance first.

Remember to be friendly with everyone. Stay away from people who seem to **gossip**, pick on other classmates, or make rude comments. The last thing anyone needs is a friend who makes others feel badly about themselves.

Making and keeping friends can be easy if you just follow a few simple rules.

Rule #1

Be kind to your friends and appreciate them for who they are.

Rule #2

Help cheer up your friends when they feel sad.

Rule #3

Make new friends and introduce them to your old friends.

Rule #4

Do not gossip about your friends, or anyone else's friends.

Super Social Tip

We have all been left out at some time. Don't be that friend. Always make your friends feel welcome.

11

Throughout school, you will meet people who enjoy being your friend. But you will also meet people who want to hurt you for their own enjoyment. Dealing with **bullying** can be painful and difficult. You need to have your own personal means of dealing with it. Find people you know you can trust to help you.

Keep open lines of communication with your parents, teachers, or other trusted grown-ups. Tell them if you are being hurt by a bully.

A bully is not just someone who hurts you physically. Bullying can be teasing, gossiping, and laughing at someone. Cruel comments disguised as jokes are also forms of bullying.

Standing by and watching someone being bullied is the same thing as being a bully. You must step in and stop it.

Bullying does not usually happen when someone is alone. It occurs most often when other people are around. If you witness bullying, it is your job to help the **victim** and stop it. The best way to deal with it is to tell a grown-up. You are not tattling if you are reporting someone being hurt either physically or **emotionally**. This makes you an **upstander** instead of a bystander.

Using technology is another scary way that people bully others. One mean comment or unflattering picture can be spread around a school in a matter of seconds. If you receive anything that can be seen as **cyber-bullying**, do not forward it or show it to other people. Immediately show it to a trusted adult.

SOCIAL SOLUTIONS

You will face many unique and challenging situations. Here are just a few to get you thinking about what you could do.

Everyone got invited to a party and I was left out.

This can be a very painful feeling when you find out you are not included. The most important thing to remember is that there will be lots of other parties. Try not to get mad at the person who is having the party or the friends that are going. Hold your head up high and remember there will be lots of parties to go to in the years ahead. Seek out other friends. Do your best to never leave someone out. You know how bad it can feel.

I made my friend mad and I don't know how to fix it.

Sometimes we hurt our friends without meaning to do it. The best thing to do is to tell your friend you understand you hurt her and apologize. Your friend may need a couple of days to cool off, but most likely you will be forgiven.

I have a friend who tells me what I can and cannot do and who I can be friends with.

This friend is not really a friend. He is trying to control you. Tell this person you think it is time to spend some time apart and find different friends.

My best friend has a new friend, and I am not sure where I fit in.

Your best friend is still your friend. There is nothing wrong with making new friends. Try to get to know this new person. The worst thing you can do is get mad or act jealous. You should also take this time to find new friendships for yourself. A person can never have too many friends!

I did something really embarrassing at school and everyone saw me do it.

We have all done something embarrassing in public. The best way to deal with it is to laugh a little at yourself and forget it. Everyone else will forget quickly too. Just remember not to laugh at someone else who is in the same situation.

Not every kid in school is going to be your friend and that is okay. Find a couple of good friends you can trust, get involved in activities that interest you, and seek out ways you can be a good friend. Always treat others with respect and kindness and people will do the same for you!

GLOSSARY

bullying (BUL-ee-ing): scaring, teasing, or hurting someone weaker than you

conversation (kon-vur-SAY-shuhn): talk with another person

cyber-bullying (SYE-bur BUL-ee-ing): scaring, teasing, or hurting someone using technology, such as a smartphone or computer

emotionally (i-MOH-shuh-nuhl-ee): acting in a way that shows strong feelings such as happiness or anger

gossip (GOSS-ip): talking about someone or telling stories about someone that are hurtful

hobbies (HOB-eez): enjoyable activities people do for fun

nervous (NUR-vuhss): feeling unsure or a little scared

upstander (UP-stan-dur): a person who takes action when they witness bullying

victim (VIK-tuhm): a person who is hurt or attacked by another person

INDEX

WEBSITES TO VISIT

pbskids.org/itsmylife/friends/index.html

www.stopbullying.gov/

kid.lifetips.com/cat/8874/friendship-tips/index.html

ABOUT THE AUTHOR

Meg Greve lives in Chicago with her husband Tom, and her two children, Madison and William. The whole family works hard to be a friend to everyone they meet!

Meet The Author!
www.meetREMauthors.com